MEDIC
AND PROPERTIES OF
FRUIT

MEDICINAL USES AND PROPERTIES OF FRUIT

Compiled and Edited
by
Christopher N Burchett

PILGRIMS PUBLISHING
◆ Varanasi ◆

MEDICINAL USES AND PROPERTIES OF FRUIT

Compiled and Edited by
Christopher N Burchett

Published by:
PILGRIMS PUBLISHING

An imprint of:
PILGRIMS BOOK HOUSE
(Distributors in India)
B 27/98 A-8, Nawabganj Road
Durga Kund, Varanasi-221010, India
Tel: 91-542- 2314060,
Fax: 91-542- 2312456
E-mail: pilgrims@satyam.net.in
Website: www.pilgrimsbooks.com

Layout & Cover design by Asha Mishra

ISBN: 81-7769-623-8

*Printed in India at Pilgrim Press Pvt. Ltd. Lalpur
Varanasi*

MEDICINAL USES OR PROPERTIES OF FRUITS

This small book about the usefulness of fruit in our everyday lives is an attempt to bring to light some of the more obscure properties of fruits that would normally remain for most of us totally unknown and thus automatically ignored. Fruit of various kinds have been known to our ancestors for thousands of years. They used them for a variety of purposes. They were an easily available source of food as they wandered through the forests in search of their daily fare. They provided them with suitable offerings to their Gods and deities. And as time went on they found them very productive when they introduced them as cures for various ailments. References to them are found in all ancient literature from the Vedas to the Bible etc. These references so highly praise these gifts of the Gods that it is obvious that we should pay a lot more attention to them and allow them to play the important role in our lives that they were meant to do.

Of course not all of them will be as easily available as others as they come from different climes and are available in different seasons. Some you may not have even heard of before. But with the world growing smaller everyday and people in larger numbers travelling far abroad to spend their leisure time it is most probable that they will come across some of them along the way. So it is always useful to know about their properties beforehand for, who knows when they may prove really useful when nothing else is available. Also these tidbits will help you know what and when to eat them or whether they are suitable to your constitution or not.

We all know how nice it is to have the fresh fruit basket or bowl standing on our dining table or sideboard available twenty-four hours a day for those who need a bite in between or just after meals or even just want to skip a meal and enjoy a simple banana or apple. Oh how these fresh fruits bring a breath of fresh air into our mundane and boring lives! Their appearance is so healthy and their aroma so pleasant it is hard to imagine a healthy life without them. As the old adage says 'An apple a day keeps the doctor away'. But is it only apples that are beneficial? We hope to show you that there is a whole gamut of fruit, common and uncommon, some seasonal and some available almost twelve months of the year that all have something to offer us other than a few minutes of pleasure.

There are some fruits that are common to all countries and others found either only in the tropics or warmer climes and some that are only available in the more temperate areas. All have something in common:— they are highly beneficial to all of us. There are many myths and stories that revolve around fruit, the most famous being most probably Eve and the forbidden fruit of the Garden of Eden commonly believed to be the apple. But of course this apple may mean something different to all of us, depending from where and how we look at it.

The ancients of India, the Rishis and Maharishis, were reputed to have lived on a diet of fruit alone. Even today fruit is used during fasting periods by Hindus almost universally as being fare fit only for the Gods. The Muslims too, at the end of each day during the month of Ramadan, stop their fast at sunset by first taking dates, the favoured fruit of their prophet Mohammed. Christians too, especially those in Europe, have plenty of fruit on their tables during the Christmas period That too, includes dates and figs, the fruits of the land of their Lord Jesus Christ.

Now one has to ask oneself whether it is only for taste alone or does the use of fruits especially at times when we are likely to overeat or overindulge ourselves have another hidden and more scientific meaning? There certainly is enough evidence to make us believe that these traditions handed down generation after generation for thousands of years must have a deeper truth involved somewhere. Even the most primitive cultures of pre-historic times must have used the fruits and berries that they found during their wanderings and became aware of the beneficial as well as the harmful properties that they possessed.

AMLA-GOOSEBERRY-
MYROBALAN

Phyllanthus amarus *Schum. & Thonn.* P. niruri *auct. non Linn.* (Euphorbiaceae*)*

Phyllanthus emblica Linn. *Emblica officinalis* Gaertn. (*Euphorbiaceae*) Tree Herb **Kizhanelli Sanskrit—Bhumyamlaki; Hindi—Jar-amla.**

Amla—ref. Jaminiya Upanishad, Chhandogya and others for medicinal value, also all Ayurvedic texts. Other Sanskrit names: Amlaka, Adiphala, Dhatri; Hindi—Amla

Amla, Myrobalan, Indian Gooseberry (Hindi— Avelah, **Sanskrit**—Amlaka, Amlaki)

Powerfully diuretic, de-obstruent, and astringent. Used in genito-urinary affections, dropsy and jaundice. Root given in menorrhagia. It is one of the most important medicinal plants, with hundreds of applications of all plant parts. A number of indigenous medicinal preparations of India contain one part of the plant or another.

Amla, Dhatribala, Nelli Gooseberry

Linctus or Jam (Avaleha, Lehya, Paka, Prasha, or Khanda)

This is a typical Ayurvedic preparation. Generally the powder or paste of the main drug, (1 part), sugar or crystal sugar (4 parts), jaggery, (2 parts) and liquid, like decoction or the juice of the drug (4 parts) are taken and cooked over fire. When the recipe becomes semi solid in consistency, the powder of the mentioned drugs should be added as *prakshepa* and stirred well. Then the recipe should be taken out from the fire, allowed to cool, and honey should be mixed. This linctus should be stored in a ghee smeared earthen or porcelain jar. If ghee or oil and the paste of drugs like *amala*, white pumpkin are mentioned, then first of all ghee or oil is to be heated and the paste is to be fried. Thereafter, liquid, jaggery etc., drugs should be added and cooked according to the procedure. Perhaps *Chyavana Prasha* is the best preparation of linctus. It is an excellent tonic, which is rich in *amalaki* (*Emblica officinalis*). It is useful in curing chronic lung diseases, like chronic bronchitis, tuberculosis, cough and asthma.

The Indian Gooseberry or Amla as it is more commonly known has provided humankind with its magical properties for thousands of years. Ayurveda has a large amount of literature dealing with this fruit and it is a common ingredient in many of its medicines and tonics. The fruit is abundantly available during the winter. It has great rejuvenating properties and is the main ingredient of 'Chyavanprash' one of the most well known and frequently used natural tonics in the ancient Indian medical system.

Qualities: the amla fruit is the same size as that of a lemon. It is pale green in colour and has vertical lines on its outer rind. Its taste is somewhat acidic and to some extent acrid. It is delicious and astringent. It vitalises hair and increases semen. It improves the eyesight and purifies the blood. Its efficacy extends to removing excesses of the three humours or 'doshas' namely wind, bile and mucus. It is considered suitable to people of all ages at all times of the year and under all circumstances.

Being the largest source of Vitamin 'C' it increases the body's resistance powers against all diseases.

Analysis of Contents

Water	81.2%
Protein	0.5%
Fat	0.1%
Carbohydrates	14.1%
Fibrous elements	3.4%
Calcium	0.05%
Phosphorus	0.02%
Iron	1.02mg/ 100gm
Vitamin 'C'	600mg/ 100gm

It also contains gallic acid and albumin. Amla retains its Vitamin 'C' content for a long time. When it is dried in the shade its Vitamin 'C' content increases. The dehydrated amla gives 2400 to 2600mg of Vitamin 'C' per 100 grams. The daily human requirement of Vitamin 'C' is 75mg., which may be easily procured if a little powder of amla or its juice is taken. The Vitamin 'C' contained in one amla fruit is more than that contained in 16 bananas or three oranges.

Use: Taking its juice is considered one of the easiest ways to take advantage of its multiple properties.

This can be obtained with the help of a juicer after cutting into small pieces and removing the seeds. Or alternatively you may shred the fruit and squeeze the pulp through a fine cloth; it may also be obtained by crushing and pounding the fruit in a stone basin. To cut the fruit into small pieces you should use a stainless steel knife rather than an iron one. The quality of amla deteriorates when it comes into contact with iron.

Its juice when taken in the morning on an empty stomach is very beneficial. As amla tastes very acrid it cannot be eaten in sufficient quantities thus drinking its juice is preferable for meeting the daily requirements. Its juice cleanses the mouth and restores the normal taste. If one wishes a small amount of honey or 'gur' (jaggery) may be added to make it more palatable. It may be stated that in its juice form it is more beneficial than in any other preparation.

Benefits: Amla or its juice is very useful in uric troubles. Drinking its fresh juice for two to three months is helpful in conditions of sterility and semen weakness. It is a sure remedy for eye weakness and deafness. It is also very helpful in conditions of constipation, blood impurities, dyspepsia, and jaundice etc. it gives relief in weakness of the nerves and heart.

APPLE

Protein content 0.2gm/ 100gm

Believed to have originated in the Caucasus Mountains it is now found universally throughout the world. It has been known in India for centuries and is abundantly available during the moths of August and September. Due to different climatic conditions in different parts of the world where it is now grown the apple is now easily available the whole year round.

Qualities: The apple has a sweet-sour taste. It is constipating, nourishing and easily digestible. It appeases bile and wind conditions, cures dyspepsia and strengthens the intestines. Its pectin content relieves cough and helps in eliminating toxic elements from the body. It is very useful in decreasing acidity in the stomach. It vitalises the heart, the brain, the liver and the stomach. It works as an appetiser and improves the quality of the blood.

Analysis of Contents

Water	85.9%
Protein	0.3%
Fat	0.1%
Carbohydrates	9.5%
Minerals	0.4%
Calcium	0.01%
Phosphorus	0.02%
Iron	1.7mg/100gm
Vitamin 'B'	40 I U/100gm
Vitamin 'C'	Trace

It also contains a small amount of copper.

Use: Fresh apple juice is very convenient for consumption. Apples may also be masticated and eaten raw providing good exercise to both the teeth and gums. The use of juice is considered by many to be more beneficial.

Dr. J H Kellogg recommended Apple juice in cases of jaundice, and he also stated that it was a good disinfectant for both the stomach and intestines. Recognised as having natural laxative qualities it should be noted that its pectin content checks diarrhoea.

Apple juice gives relief in cases of debility, in weakness of the nervous system, kidney stone,

11

acidity, indigestion, headache, biliousness, asthma and dysentery. The slight acid content exerts an antiseptic influence upon germs present in the mouth and teeth, when it is taken by chewing sufficiently. It is considered as a natural teeth protector and its consumption is recommended in all dental problems.

BANANA

Rich in Vitamin 'B'

Bananas play a positive role in producing sexual hormones. They also help to reduce mental stress. This is due to the high quantity of potassium that is present there. This eases the proper secretion of hormones especially sexual ones. Once called by Mahatma Gandhi as the fruit of the poor man, banana is commonly used on the sub-continent not only as a fruit but also as a vegetable. The un-ripe banana is used as a vegetable to help in cases of diarrhoea where it is commonly used as a first line medicine to combat the problem.

BEL

(*AEGLE MARMELOS*—LINN. CORR)

(Rutacae)—Tree also known as *Koovalam, Shreephal, Vilvam* and *Baci fruit*

Beneficent Parts: The fruit, root-bark, leaves, rind of the ripe fruit and flowers. Contains a bitter principle, volatile oils pectin and tannin. The wood-ash is rich in minerals and phosphates. Valuable in habitual constipation, and dyspepsia etc., it is also useful in chronic diarrhoea and dysentery of children. Decoction of the root and stem-bark is used in the palpitation of the heart. Leaf-juice is reported to have multifarious and medicinal uses, including control of diabetes.

Sanskrit—Viva—References innumerable in the Brihatrayi and other texts and also in Vedic literature, Epics, and Puranas etc. **Hindi**—Bel

The 'Bel' is a native of India. It has been considered a medicinal herb for centuries. Round in shape it resembles a wood apple with its hard outer rind. The size of a tennis ball it is sweet and contains a lot of seeds.

Qualities: The Bel is sweet, light, digestive, a kindler of gastric fire and slightly constipating. It destroys intestinal worms, stops nausea, vomiting and relieves cramps of the stomach muscles. Ayurveda considers it 'Tridoshar' i.e., a remedy for the three systematic disturbances viz., mucous, wind and bile.

Analysis of Contents

Water	84.0%
Protein	0.7%
Fat	0.7%
Carbohydrates	16.2%
Tannin	9.0 to 20.0%
Vitamin 'C'	7.6mg/ 100gm

It also contains a small amount of Vitamin 'B_1', Vitamin 'B_2', niacin, calcium, phosphorus and iron.

Use: The pulp of the ripe Bel may be taken directly or it may be taken in its juice form. This will provide you with a wonderful drink in the summer months but a lot of care must be taken to separate the seeds, which tend to remain.

Benefits: The medicinal value of bel is principally dependent upon the tannin it contains. In digestive disorders, and chronic dysentery, Bel is regarded as an invaluable remedy in bowel complaints and cholera also. It has also been stated that Bel is a nutritious blood purifier too and that 50gm of bel mixed with hot water and sugar, taken 2-3 times every day helps to purify the blood and eradicate impurities.

According to Dr. R L Dutt bel juice is very valuable in bowel complaints and cholera. Dr. G Price of Bihar tells us that that it is also a very good laxative. Other doctors of eminence have stated that it is a good blood purifier. Bel may be taken as a juice or taken in its crystallised form for a whole variety of stomach complaints. Bel also plays a very important part in the religious life of the Hindus and is considered by them to be one of the favoured fruits of the lord Shiva.

COCONUT
COCOS NUCIFERA LINN.

(Arecaceae) Tree

Deerghavriksha, Dridhabala, Kera, Kuberaka, Narikela, Rasayanataru, Sadaphal, Thengu, Trinaraj, Tunga.

So many synonyms for a tree in Sanskrit, each indicating a different quality of the tree, are very rare in the plant kingdom, and show how important the tree has been from ancient times. The coconut tree can grow to a height of 35 to 45 metres. (A 45-metre tall coconut tree is believed to be 125 years old and gives a normal yield like any other younger tree of its kind.) For a long time coconut research in India was oriented towards producing short, dwarf trees capable of very high yields and this work has been a remarkable success. High yielding dwarfs have now largely replaced the old tall varieties.

The coconut tree yields food, medicines, liquor (which can be used for body-building or intoxication, depending on the quantity consumed), oil, sugar and building materials. Because of the multifarious benefits given by the tree to humanity, it is rightly called *Kalpakataru* (after the legendary tree of heaven, which grants any desire to the asker) and *Punyataru* (the Holy tree).

The expressed milk juice of the coconut kernel contains sugar, resin, albumin, tartaric acid, and oil globules finely dispersed. The coconut oil itself when expressed from the dried kernel called "Copra", contains caprylic acid, myristic acid, stearic acid and glycerides. The ashes of the burnt coconut wood and leaves contain abundance of potash. The coconut toddy (Neera) tapped from the flowers contains bodybuilding sugars, enzymes and fats. Tender coconut water (also wrongly called 'coconut milk') is prescribed by Ayurvedic Physicians as a drink for heart patients, and those suffering from dysentery. Coconut water reduces the harmful effects of mercury poisoning and hastens recovery. Coconut kernel increases semen, regulates irregular menses, and fresh coconut toddy in moderate quantities improves health and vitality. The growing tender shoot of the coconut tree ground with molasses, and eaten regularly for a few days, cures women of their menstrual haemorrhages and vaginal discharge of mucus. When the root of the coconut tree is ground and boiled with water and the filtered decoction is administered internally, even very serious stomach ailments are cured. In fact the culinary, pharmaceutical and industrial uses of coconut oil are well known the world over.

The sweet toddy obtained by tapping the coconut palm flowers contains between 12 and 16 percent sucrose. *Gur* (unrefined, solidified mass of sugar, grey-brown to blackish in colour, containing mainly sucrose) is manufactured by concentrating the toddy from the coconut tree as also from other palms such as Palmyra (*Borassus flabellifer*), the date palm (*Phoenix sylvestris*) and Saro (*Caryota urens*). The date palm, which grows wild in India should not be confused with the real date yielding palm, *Pheonix dactylifera*.

Narikela—Innumerable starting from Vedic literature. All Ayurvedic texts.

The early home of the coconut is thought to have been the islands of the Indian and pacific oceans. It is now cultivated in many parts of the world where climatic conditions are favourable.

Qualities: the water found in the green coconut is cool, exhilarant, nutritious and diuretic. It moderates the colour of urine and quenches the thirst. When the coconut is not ripe and the formation of the inner kernel has not taken place, its water is less sweet, sour or to some extent astringent. Its water becomes sweet as soon as the formation of the inner kernel takes place. Sugar contained in its water is quickly absorbed. It is safe because it is naturally sterilised and hence free from bacteria.

Analysis of Contents

Water	95.5%
Protein	3.5%
Fat	0.2%
Sodium	105mg/100gm
Potassium	312mg/100gm
Calcium	29mg/100gm
Magnesium	30mg/100gm
Phosphorus	37mg/100gm
Iron	0.1mg/100gm
Copper	0.04mg/100gm
Sulphur	24mg/100gm
Chlorine	183mg/100gm

Vitamin 'B' complex (Food Science March 1958 p.66)

Niacin	0.64mg/ 100gm
Pantothenic acid	0.52mg/ 100gm
Biotin	0.02mg/ 100gm
Riboflavin	0.01mg/ 100gm

Pyrodoxine very small amount/ 100gm

Green coconut water is a good source of mineral salts and Vitamin 'B' complex (Council of Scientific Industrial Research—The Wealth of India Vol. II p.278)

Use: Green coconut water is rich in the above-mentioned elements and vitamins. As the nut develops and becomes ripe and yellow, it gradually loses many of its nutritional values. So the water of only green and tender coconuts is beneficial to drink. It should be used immediately. Adding a few drops of lemon juice to the water can compensate the Vitamin 'C' deficiency in coconut.

Benefits: As green coconut water is diuretic, it is very efficacious in urine troubles and kidney stones. It is very useful in cholera, the vomiting and diarrhoea associated with cholera leads to dehydration of the body very quickly causing the body to lose valuable minerals and salts; this can prove fatal if not quickly attended to. It is in cases like these that coconut water proves to be of great assistance as it provides the necessary minerals and salts as well as necessary fluids to the body. Being antibacterial it also extirpates the cholera germs from the intestines. Scientists from the school of tropical medicines believe that coconut water is rich in natural potassium and is superior to injections of the same whilst treating cases of cholera.

The Vitamin 'B' complex contained in coconut water strengthens the heart and vitalises the nerves and the digestive system.

Coconut oil that is extracted from the soft kernel that eventually forms within the coconut shell is a good cooking agent and also a good massage oil and hair tonic. Its neutral effects make it a good base for use with other herbs and thus in the absence of sesame oil it is often suggested in combinations of medicinal oils.

CUSTARD APPLE
Custard Apple or Sitaphala—***Annona***

***reticulata* Linn. (*Annonaceae*)**

Small tree *Atha*, *Sitaphal*, *Subha*, *Custard apple*, *Ylang Ylang*

All parts of the custard apple may be used especially its leaves, bark, seeds and fruit. It is vermicide and insecticide; the root is a violent purgative. The leaf paste when applied to unhealthy ulcers proves very effective. Seeds cause abortion. Leaves are useful in cutting short fits of hysteria and fainting. Fruit along with ginger is administered in cases of mental aberration. Bark internally used in depression of spirit, asthma and fever.

FIG

The fig is another fruit of antiquity. Copious references to the fig are to be found in Biblical texts as well as those of ancient Greece and Rome. It is a nutritious fruit with sweet soothing laxative qualities. The iron content found in figs is easily digested and therefore completely assimilated in the body. Cool delicious and heavy, they control bile excretions and relieve flatulence. They eliminate impurities in the blood.

Analysis of Contents

Water	80.8%
Protein	3.5%
Fat	0.2%
Carbohydrates	18.7%
Minerals	0.7%
Calcium	0.06%
Phosphorus	0.03%
Iron	1.2mg/100gm
Vitamin 'A'	270 I U/100gm

The fig contains plenty of sodium, potassium, calcium, iron, copper, magnesium, phosphorus, sulphur and chlorine. Fresh figs are rich in vitamin 'A'. They also contain Vitamins 'B' and 'C' in moderate proportions. In comparison with fresh figs dry figs contain 3-4 times more sugar and minerals when taken weight for weight. This is a dextrose and fruit sugar. In some varieties the dextrose content is almost 60%. (Heber W Youngken)

Use: They may be taken as a juice or eaten as they are. In the absence of fresh figs the dried ones are equally effective. You may also soak the dried figs making them smooth and soft and also activating the enzymes at the same time. You may also extract juice from dried figs treated in this way. The water that is used to soak the dried figs should not be discarded and may be used to dilute thick juice.

Benefits: The juice of fresh figs is diuretic and therefore alleviates uric problems. It also keeps the liver, stomach and the intestines in an efficient working mode. It removes constipation, fatigue as well as weakness. It can also relieve violent fits of coughing. Children and pregnant women are highly benefited and gain vigour by the regular use off figs.

GRAPES

Another universally known fruit of antiquity, probably more famous for it use in wine manufacture. According to Charaka (The famous Rishi of Ayurveda) grapes are sweet, stimulative, soothing, and beneficial to the throat, hair, skin and eyes. They also act as an appetiser. Ripe grapes are oily, diuretic, aphrodisiac, cool and refreshing. They help to eliminate thirst, burning sensations, fever, asthma, leprosy, tuberculosis, irregular menstruation, voice trouble, vomiting, obesity, oedema, chronic jaundice (hepatitis) and other disorders. They decrease gastric acidity.

Sushrut another great Ayurvedacharya (teacher of Ayurveda), is of the opinion that grapes help to retain youth and prevents aging. He states that grapes are nutritive and a preventative for wasting diseases (Sushrut Samhita Ch. 46). They sooth the burning sensations in the stomach and as they are productive in digestive problems they also help to alleviate the formation of excess gas.

Grapes relive uric troubles, burning sensations in the bladder and kidney stones. The have been found of value in arthritis, irregular and painful menstruation and bleeding.

Analysis of Contents

Water	85.5%
Protein	0.8%
Fat	7.1%
Carbohydrates	10.2%
Phosphorus	0.02%
Iron	0.04mg/100gm
Vitamin 'A'	15 I.U/ 100gm
Vitamin 'B$_2$'	10mg/100gm
Niacin	0.3mg/ 100gm
Vitamin 'C'	10mg/ 100gm

Raw grapes contain a lot of acid elements and less sugar but on ripening the sugar content rises appreciably. The sugar found in grapes is formed almost by glucose. The proportion of glucose in grapes is much more in comparison to other fruit in equal weight. In some varieties the sugar content is as high as 50% (Henry Sherman). The glucose in grapes is predigested sugar and is easily absorbed into the body.

Though iron is scanty it is easy to assimilate and is therefore useful in anaemia. A number of investigators have found that only 300ml of grape-juice can successfully arrest the progress of anaemia.

Malic, citric and tartaric acids contained in grapes purify the blood and stimulate the activity of the bowels as well as the kidneys. Vagbhat, another renowned Ayurveda expert had also come to similar conclusions about the efficacy of grapes (Vagbhat Sutrasthana 6-106).

Use: Though grapes can easily be taken in their natural form, pure grape juice has a greater medicinal value. A sufficient amount of grapes can be taken only in the juice form.

Benefits: Grapes, if taken daily, are very good for relieving constipation. They bring relief in piles. They have a soothing effect on the excess excretion of bile and burning sensations in the stomach. Grape juice brings good results in those suffering from weakness, debility, stagnated weight, dryness of skin, dimness of sight and burning sensations in the body. Taking grape juice for a few days removes undesirable heat from the body as the blood is cleansed and cooled.

Dr. J H Kellogg once related to an incident where a group of soldiers suffering from chronic dysentery were stationed near a vineyard. They drank grape juice and were cured of all symptoms of dysentery.

Ms Johanna Brandt has made mention in her book 'The Grape Cure' of her own personal experience with grape juice when she was diagnosed as having a stomach cancer. She found that a regimen, which included the use of grape juice, brought amazing results. Always remember that whenever you are suffering with a serious complaint the advice of a recognised Naturopath is essential before undertaking any form of self-treatment.

GUAVA—Psidium guajava L.

Hindi—Amrud

Contains more Vitamin 'C' than any other fruit excepting the Indian Gooseberry (amla). Though not indigenous to the sub-continent guava was known in ancient India. There are two varieties one white and the other pink, the white variety being sweeter than the other. In India guavas from Prayag (Allahabad) and Varanasi both in the State of Uttar Pradesh, are considered to be the best.

The guava is a palatable, astringent and sweet fruit. It promotes semen. It is beneficial in constipation, it is cool and it checks the flow of excess bile, it also works as an appetiser. It has been stated to cure delusion and hysteria, destroys intestinal worms and quenches thirst. It is said to give relief in insanity and it also eliminates constipation.

Analysis of Contents

Water	76.1%
Protein	1.5%
Fat	0.2%
Carbohydrates	14.5%
Calcium	0.01%
Phosphorus	0.04%
Iron	1mg/100gm
Vitamin 'C'	300mg/100gm

As mentioned previously that other than the Indian Gooseberry it contains more vitamin 'C' than any other fruit, but when it is over ripe and soft its Vitamin 'C' potency decreases. The rind and neighbouring flesh contain the most Vitamin 'C'.

Uses: The guava can be taken by directly chewing it well but to obtain more nutrients it should be taken in the form of juice. Every 100ml contains 70-170 milligrams of Vitamin 'C'.

Benefits: Guava is beneficial in constipation, blood impurities, leprosy and other diseases.

JAMUN-Black Plum—Syzygium cumini (Linn.) Skeels

Eugenia jambolana Lamk. (Myrtaceae) *Jambu, Jambul, Jamun Black plum*

The leaves are astringent, their juice is a useful remedy for dysentery with bloody discharges; it is given in two to four fluid ounce doses.

The bark is astringent; its juice is given in two to four fluid ounce doses in chronic diarrhoea, dysentery and menorrhagia; its powder is given in doses of five to ten grains, with curd in menorrhagia.

A decoction of the bark is an efficacious mouth-wash and gargle for treating spongy gums, stomatis, relaxed throat and other diseases of the mouth; a paste of the burnt bark with some bland oil is applied over burns and scalds.

The ripe fruit is astringent, stomachic, carminative, antiscorutic and diuretic; its juice is generally used in enlargement of the spleen, chronic diarrhoea and suppressed scanty urine.

The seed is astringent; it is very efficacious for diabetes mellitus and for glycosuria; it quickly reduces sugar in urine; a liquid extract of the seed is given in half to two drachm doses; a powder is made of the carefully dried fresh seed is given at first in doses of five to fifteen grains and gradually increased to forty grains; in five to ten grain doses the powder is given in diarrhoea and dysentery.

(Dastur)
Jambu—References innumerable. Medicinal properties in Ayurvedic texts, Kurmapurana.

Jamun or Jambul is as valuable in the rainy season as the mango is in summer. It is delicious, a bit sour and to some extent astringent in taste.

Analysis of Contents

Water	78.2%
Protein	0.7%
Fat	0.1%
Carbohydrates	19.7%
Calcium	0.02%
Phosphorus	0.01%
Iron	1.00mg/100gm

It contains a certain amount of Vitamin 'C' and Vitamin 'B' complex. It also contains folic acid and choline.

Use: The fruit should be soaked in cold water for an hour and the seed removed before the juice is extracted.

It is contra indicated in those who suffer from gas and should not be taken on an empty stomach. It should be eaten only after meals and milk should be avoided 3 hours before or after its consumption. It is also contra-indicated in those suffering from oedema or those with vomiting tendencies. It is completely forbidden to women just after delivery and for those observing fasts.

Benefits: Jamun juice is more effective than more expensive liver extracts in spleen and liver disorders. It activates the liver and eliminates abdominal pain; it tones up the heart and helps in the cure of anaemia it also gives relief to burning sensations in the kidney. Jamun is an excellent medicine in the treatment for gonorrhoea and diabetes. It cures indigestion, diarrhoea, dysentery, kidney stone and leprosy it also removes impurities from the blood.

LEMON AND LIME

Citrus aurantifolia (Christm.)
Swingle C. acida Roxb. (Rutaceae) Tree
Cherunarakom, The lime. **A very good source of
vitamin C. Sanskrit—Nimbuka, Jambhira—
Reference innumerable; Hindi—Kaghzi nimba.**

A few drops of fresh lime put in the eyes gradually dissolves cataract. Juice is a very refrigerant drink useful in smallpox, and fevers etc. Juice improves liver, heart and eyes etc. Leaves used in bleeding gums.

In the opinion of some lemon is nothing more than an orange with more acid and less sugar. It is indigenous to India but is now widely found all over the world. It grows in abundance in Sri Lanka, Malaysia, Mexico and the West Indies. Unripe they are green but upon ripening they turn yellow. The lemon is a must for every kitchen and has now become a universally popular culinary aid.

Qualities: regarded in Ayurveda as a very valuable fruit it is sour, warm, promoter of gastric fire, light, good for vision, pungent, and astringent. It checks the excessive flow of bile and cleanses the mouth. It dislodges phlegm (cough) and expels wind from the digestive tract. It is an aid in digestion and removes constipation too. A preventative for vomiting, throat trouble acidity and rheumatism it destroys intestinal worms. Though it is acidic to the taste it leaves alkaline residues in the body. This is one of the reasons why it is so useful in all symptoms of acidosis.

Lemon juice is a powerful anti bacterial, this has been established in experiments carried out by eminent persons in the field like Professor Cox, Dr. J H Kellogg and Dr. Wilson. They have stated that the bacteria of malaria, cholera, diphtheria, typhoid and other deadly diseases are destroyed in lemon-juice.

Analysis of Contents

Water	85.00%
Protein	1.00%
Fat	0.9%
Carbohydrates	11.1%
Fibres	1.8%

Fruit and their Medicinal Uses

Calcium	0.07%
Phosphorus	0.03%
Iron	2.3mg/100gm
Vitamin 'C'	39mg/100gm

It also contains some Vitamin 'A'. Natural vitamin 'C' is much more effective than its synthetic counterpart, that of lemon more so as it is combined with bio-flavanoids (i.e. Vitamin 'P'), in addition it also contains niacin and thiamin in small amounts.

Use: One should not take concentrated lemon juice and it should be diluted in water before taking it. Absolutely pure lemon juice contains acids that are harmful to the enamel of the teeth. The body is well cleansed if lemon juice mixed with cold water and honey is taken on an empty stomach early in the morning. Warm water may be used occasionally to get relief from constipation.

Benefits: Lemon-juice prevents or restrains influenza, malaria and colds. According to Nobel Prize winner, Professor Fanmüller, he had proved with experiments that lemon was antibacterial. These attributes should be taken advantage of especially during the monsoon in India.

Fruit and their Medicinal Uses

Lemon juice gives relief in fevers; it quenches the thirst of those suffering with diabetes. It gives immediate relief to those suffering with abdominal disorders and acts as a sedative for the nerves and heart thus allaying troublesome palpitations. It is especially appreciated for its Vitamin 'C' value. This was shown by Vasco da Gama's voyage around the Cape of Good Hope when he lost more than two thirds of his crew to scurvy. After that event the widespread use of lemons on long voyages has saved the lives of innumerable seamen.

Vitamin 'P' in lemon strengthens the blood vessels and prevents internal haemorrhage. It is therefore very useful in cases of high blood pressure, in which cerebro-vascular accidents often occur.

The most valuable ingredient of lemon, next to vitamin 'C', is citric acid, of which it contains 7.2%. Lemon also contains more potassium, which is beneficial to the heart, than apples or grapes. It also helps to maintain the health of teeth and bones and its vitamin 'C' content helps considerably in calcium metabolism. It has been used for years in cases of gout and rheumatism.

Lemon juice is a diuretic and therefore gives relief in kidney and bladder disorders. It has been used to destroy internal worms and it prevents vomiting and helps in the cure of hepatitis and other innumerable diseases.

It has proved a blessing for mountaineers, especially in cases of insufficient oxygen and difficulty in breathing. Sir Edmund Hillary is on record as admiting his that his victory over Everest was greatly due to the humble lemon.

MANGO

Rich in Vitamin 'A'

Mango helps to convert cholesterol into active sexual hormones.

Though the mango is not specifically mentioned as a medicine it is now one of the most sought after fruit. It is enjoyed throughout India simply as a fruit or in the form of milk shakes and later on as dried fruit when out of season.

In its unripe form it is used in chutanies and pickles and consumed as side dishes with most Indian food. The mango when taken with milk is also very nourishing as well.

It is also in demand throughout the world and has become very popular in the western world.

MELON

Either round or oval in shape it is most suitably grown on a sandy riverbank. Melon with white flesh is known as muskmelon and is extremely sweet, while melon with green or yellow flesh is known as watermelon, and is not as sweet as the muskmelon. Both melons belong to the same genus.

Qualities: Melon is cool and diuretic. It quenches thirst and gives a welcoming, cooling and soothing effect during hot summer days.

Analysis of Contents

Water	95.9%
Protein	0.1%
Fat	0.1%
Carbohydrates	3.9%
Calcium	0.11%
Phosphorus	0.01%
Sodium	0.01%
Iron	0.2mg/100gm
Vitamin 'A' and 'C' Trace	

As it contains predigested sugar, it provides prompt nourishment.

Use: Melon is mostly composed of water and it contains a little or no fibres. It can, therefore, be consumed either directly or in juice form.

Benefits: As the melon has a cooling effect, it soothes burning sensations in the stomach. Its mineral contents eliminate acidity from the body and it is also useful in curing constipation. It is also a powerful diuretic and can help in allaying kidney diseases. It is also very beneficial in chronic and acute cases of eczema.

As melon juice promotes mucus, one who suffers from asthma, catarrh and colds should use it discretely, or use it after slightly warming it.

ORANGE

Its origins have been traced to South China, from where it has spread to become one of the most popular fruits the world over. It is mainly popular for its sweet sour taste, juiciness and coolness. In India there are two seasons for cultivation: one from October to February and the other from March to May. In other parts of the world its cultivation takes place according to prevailing climatic conditions. Israel and Spain are famous for their production of some of the more popular varieties. In India the oranges from Nagpur in Maharastra, where they grow in abundance, are the most favoured.

Qualities: The Ayurveda also has recognised the value of oranges. They work as an appetiser, cleanse the blood, soothes bile and eliminates wind. The orange is cool and refreshing. It cleanses the mouth and is very useful in fevers. The orange also destroys intestinal worms and allays abdominal pain. It strengthens bones. In the West too naturopaths have also come to the conclusion that oranges are rich in salts especially lime and alkaline salts that counteract the tendency to acidosis. In such serious conditions as scurvy, beriberi, neuritis, anaemia, or in any condition where the tissues are bathed in acid secretions the alkaline mineral salts of fresh fruits will be of great benefit. In this respect the orange, lemon and grapefruit are invaluable.

Analysis of Contents

Water	87.8%
Protein	0.9%
Fat	0.3%
Carbohydrates	10.6%
Calcium	0.05%
Phosphorus	0.02%
Iron	0.1mg/ 100gm
Sodium	2.1mg/ 100gm
Potassium	19.7mg/ 100gm
Magnesium	12.9mg/ 100gm
Copper	0.07mg/ 100gm
Sulphur	9.3mg/ 100gm
Chlorine	3.2mg/ 100gm
Vitamin 'A'	350 I U/100gm

Vitamin 'B$_1$'   120 I.U/ 100gm
Vitamin 'C'   68mg/ 100gm

The orange is a rich source of Vitamin 'C'. the daily requirement of Vitamin 'C' can be met by taking 125-150ml of orange juice. The vitamin 'C' content of the orange is not easily destroyed because it is protected by the citric acid. Besides Vitamin 'C' the orange is blended with calcium thereby the qualities of each are increased. The white membrane, which surrounds the sections of the orange, is also an excellent source of calcium.

As orange juice contains less acid than lemon juice, it is regarded as superior to the latter. Though the citric acid contained in the orange is somewhat acidic to taste, it is an alkali forming food. After being metabolised in the tissues it leaves an alkaline residue and thus improves the vital resistance of the body. (Henry Sherman— The Science of Nutrition p.110)

Use: The orange is usually taken by chewing it or in its juice form. When there is a need to obtain a large quantity of nutrients, orange juice is preferred. Those who suffer from cold should add some warm water to orange juice before taking it. Orange juice is particularly suited to those suffering with fevers. It is recommended that to compensate the loss of liquids that four to six quarts of liquid should be consumed every day. This will help to relieve what is called the fever's fire and also to eliminate poisons through the skin and kidney as a fever is an indication of the body's wish to relieve itself from an excess of such poisons that have accumulated over a period of time. This is often caused by our lifestyles, which tend to work in opposition to more natural ways of life.

Benefits: To overcome constipation, it is sufficient to take one or two oranges before going to bed and again on rising early in the morning. Oranges are useful in asthma and other bronchial troubles.

During fevers, orange juice greatly helps in supplying the necessary nutrition to the patient. It improves digestion and acts as an appetiser. Orange juice renders the intestinal tract uninhabitable for hostile microbes and improves intestinal health. (Henry Sherman—Foods, Their Values and Management, p.72.) It increases vitality and gives relief during pregnancy to those who suffer from excessive vomiting.

A cup of orange juice provides as many calories as three quarters of a cup of milk. (J H Kellogg—The New Dietetics, p.346.)

Fruit and their Medicinal Uses

In chronic dyspepsia when food is not well digested it tends to putrefy in the digestive tract, causing gas. Orange juice helps in eliminating this condition in the stomach. It cleanses the stomach and intestinal tracts thereby increasing the digestive power of both the digestive organs.

A glass of orange juice has more Vitamin 'A', thiamine, niacin, Vitamin 'C' and more iron and potassium than a glass of milk. The amount of food value found in one large orange is about equal to that found in a large slice of bread, with the added benefit that it is immediately assimilated into the body whereas the bread will pass through the hours' long process of digestion. This is why oranges are so beneficial in strengthening and revitalising invalids and feeble persons, as well as maintaining a healthy balance in healthy people.

Orange juice is indispensable for bottle-feeding babies. Its use goes a long way to prevent scurvy, rickets and pellagra. The acid and sugar that they contain aid digestion and generally stimulate and increase the activity of glands in the stomach. It is felt in some quarters that orange juice is capable of serving more useful purposes in the body than any other fruit. It must also be noted that the sweeter the orange the greater its food value is. It is sure that as people become more conscious of the nutritive values of natural foods, fruits like the orange will become far more appreciated not only for their food value but for their medicinal values too.

PAPAYA Carica papaya L.

Hindi—Papeeta

Papaya is a tree that resembles a palm and has seven lobed leaves. Its fruit is yellow orange when ripe and has the appearance of a melon hence it having been called by some the *Melon Tree*. The seeds of the ripe fruit are black and resemble peppercorns and are bitter in taste. It is indigenous to the Americas and the West Indies and found its way to the rest of the world in the 16th century. It is a cheap, easily available sweet fruit. It grows between the months of February and March and May and October. The unripe fruit is green and can be used almost as a vegetable and in this form is often recommended as staple food for those suffering from jaundice.

Qualities: The ripe papaya is a delicious, heavy, warm, oily, laxative and anti-bilious. It increases virility, is beneficial to both the heart and liver, and is also said to alleviate insanity. The papaya also helps to check spleen enlargement (splenomegaly) and is a good medicine for constipation and urinary disorders. Its fruit, juice, seeds and leaves are all beneficial in one way or another.

Analysis of Contents

Water	89.6%
Protein	0.5%
Fat	0.1%
Carbohydrates	9.5%
Minerals	0.4%
Calcium	0.01%
Phosphorus	0.01%
Iron	0.4mg/100gm
Vitamin 'A'	2020 I U/100gm
Vitamin 'C'	46 to 136mg/ 100gm

Nearly one half of the sugar in the papaya is constituted of glucose and the other half mainly by fruit sugar (fructose). As a source of Vitamin 'A' among fruits, papaya ranks next to mango; Vitamin 'C' in papaya increases with maturity. Experiments in Hawaii showed that in extremely raw conditions it contained 32mg, green 40 to 72mg, half-ripe 53-95mg and the ripe papaya 68 to 136mg of Vitamin 'C' per 100gm.

The sugar and vitamin 'C' content of the papaya are highest during the months of May through October. Papaya also contains Vitamins 'B_1' and 'B_2' as well as niacin. The white (milky) secretion of raw papaya contains the digestive enzyme papain in significant quantities. Papain is a protein- digesting enzyme.

Use: Raw papaya can be used in juice form. The ripe papaya can be taken in its natural form. Juice can also be taken from it by adding a little milk or water to it in a mixer or blender. The juice is delicious and refreshing. Papaya is also a top-notch tea for digestive disorders. It contains enzymes for healthy digestion and assimilation of nutrients; this includes the powerful papain to digest proteins, pepsin to digest vegetables, an enzyme to digest milk-proteins and one for starches. It counters acidity, which in turn eases gastrointestinal distress, acid reflux, indigestion and constipation. It was a well-known 16th century remedy for gastrointestinal disorders.

Benefits: The raw papaya juice is useful in expelling round worms from the digestive tract. It is very effective in liver problems, and it helps to secure proper menstrual flow. Ayurvedic experts have recognised the papain content of the fruit as being a remedy for abdominal disorders. It is considered to be a good medicine for dysentery, hyperacidity, dyspepsia and constipation. It has been proved very effective in cases of anaemia and splenomegaly. In addition to papain papaya contains enzymes such as arginine (for male fertility) and fibrin (necessary for blood coagulation). Papaya contains an alkaloid carpain, which is good for the health of the heart. Papaya cleanses the lymph system and fights infections. As weight loss problems are often related to digestive difficulties, gastrointestinal distress, constipation and waste stagnation, a good way to weight regulation would be to put all these in order. Papaya is one of the most natural ways to go about this. It may be eaten as a vegetable, a fruit, a juice or even as a tea. It is one of those natural wonders that most of us still have to explore.

Dr. Lytton Bernard has claimed rejuvenating properties for papaya from the control of ageing. To cleanse the body completely the easiest way is to consume about 200ml of its juice daily. Taking its juice alternately with cucumber juice every hour may speed up this process.

Because of the different types of enzymes found in the papaya it has been recommended as a supplementary treatment for cancer. After treatment with antibiotics, use of the papaya juice will speed up the restoration of the friendly symbiotic bacteria in the stomach and intestines, which will have been destroyed by the drugs.

The papaya is also a diuretic and is therefore beneficial in kidney disorders. The ripe fruit is a sure remedy for constipation. It gives relief in asthma too. Some Ayurveda experts believe that papaya causes heat in the body. They therefore advise that it should be avoided during pregnancy or whilst suffering with a fever. Its seeds are used for quenching thirst and for destroying intestinal worms. A poultice made from the leaves of the plant is beneficial in neuralgia (nerve-pain) and elephantiasis (The Council of Industrial Research, 'The Wealth of India' Vol. II p.79).

PETHA

Benincasa hispida (Thunb.) Cogn. *B. cerifera* Savi (*Cucurbitaceae*)

Climbing herb *Kooshmandam, Kumbalam, White gourd melon, Ash gourd melon*

Kushmanda—Ref. Ashtangahridayam Chapter XII, Hindi—Petha

Leaves contain blood-coagulant principle and the leaf juice causes immediate stoppage of bleeding from cuts and wounds. The fresh juice of the fruit is a specific in haemoptysis and other haemorrhages from internal organs. Juice is also useful in phthisis and insanity, epilepsy and other nervous diseases. A good anti-dote for vegetable poisons, mercurial and alcoholic poisonings. Many other medical uses.

PINEAPPLE

Ananas comosus (**Linn.**) **Merr**. (Bromeliaceae)
Shrub *Kaita chakka*

Bahunetra Ref. Kerala Ayurvedic texts.
Sanskrit—Anannasa; Hindi—Anannas

The pineapple is believed to have originated in
the rain forests of Brazil and was introduced into
Europe by Columbus. From there it spread else-
where. There are records of the Portuguese having brought it to India. It is freely grown in India
and is available during the months of July, August, September, October and November. The
pineapples grown in Myanmar (Burma), Malaysia and the Philippine Islands are considered to
be of excellent quality.

Qualities: Ayurveda has brought to light many
of the properties of pineapple. The ripe fruit is a
diuretic. It is delicious and digestive. It destroys

intestinal worms and soothes bile. It expels gas and is beneficial to the heart and effective in abdominal disorders, jaundice and anaemia.

Although the nutritive value of pineapple is known all over the world and its taste and flavour much liked, its contribution to herbal medicine is not so well recognised. Pineapple contains small quantities of Bromelin. The juice contains a proteins digestive principle, which acts both in acid or alkaline intestinal secretions. The leaf juice is a powerful purgative, anthelmintic and vermicide. The juice of the ripe fruit is antiscorbutic, diuretic, diaphoretic, aperient, and refrigerant and helps in the digestion of albuminous substances. Juice of the unripe fruit is a powerful diuretic, anthelmintic and emmenagogue. In large doses, it can cause abortion.

Analysis of Contents

Water	86.5%
Protein	0.6%
Fat	0.1%
Sugar	12.0%
Calcium	0.12%
Phosphorus	0.01%
Iron	0.9mg/100gm
Vitamin 'A'	60 I U/100gm

Vitamin 'B$_2$'	120 I.U/ 100gm
Vitamin 'C'	63mg/ 100gm

The pineapple contains 12% sugar. About 45 of its sugar is constituted of glucose while 7.5% is cane sugar. 87% of its acids are formed by citric acid and 13% by malic acid. Both of these acids are beneficial to the body.

Use: The pineapple should not be taken on an empty stomach. The upper rind and the inner-most flesh of the pineapple should be discarded. The remaining portion should be cut into pieces. Pineapple juice should be extracted from these pieces. Raw pineapple or excessively ripe pine-apple should be avoided during pregnancy.

Benefits: fresh pineapple or pineapple juice exer-cises a soothing effect on the throat. It is very useful in preventing affections of the vocal or-gans. In cases of diphtheria it is useful in remov-ing dead membranes from the throat. Experts in the field of Ayurveda have confirmed this antiviral property of the pineapple. (An Indian Dietarian— Food and Nutrition in India, p.191.) As per their opinion pineapple allays bile, destroys intestinal worms and is beneficial to the heart.

Chlorine contained in the pineapple stimulates the activity of the kidneys and helps to remove toxic elements and waste products from the body (W B Hays—Fruits Growing in India, p.221). It also gives relief to cellulitis.

PLUM

Rich in Vitamin 'A'

Plums help to convert cholesterol into active sexual hormones.

They are also a good laxitive whether eaten raw or cooked they are also preserved in the form of prunes or jam.

The plum is more commonly found in Europe and the west and is a seasonal and well liked fruit amongst all sections of society.

POMEGRANATE

Believed to have been a native of Persia and Afghanistan it has been used in India for centuries. In ancient times King Solomon had a garden exclusively of pomegranates. Previously pomegranates were imported from Afghanistan but now they also grow in India. Those grown in Gujarat are very popular and they grow during the summer.

Qualities: there are three varieties of pomegranates—sweet, sourly sweet and sourly sweet with astringent taste. Sweet pomegranates are excellent. They are delicious, light, astringent, constipating and lubricous. They increase intellect, vitalise the body and satisfy hunger. According to Ayurveda, they are '*tridoshnashak*', that is they effectively alleviate troubles in all three humours, viz. bile, wind and mucus. The pomegranate is also beneficial in thirst, burning sensations, fever, cardiac trouble, mouth disease and vocal disorders. Furthermore it helps to cure dysentery and increase blood and vitality.

Analysis of Contents

Water	78.0%
Protein	1.7%
Fat	0.1%
Carbohydrates	14.5%
Calcium	0.01%
Phosphorus	0.07%
Iron	0.3mg/100gm
Vitamin 'B$_2$'	10mg/100gm
Vitamin 'C'	16mg/100gm

The sugar content of the pomegranate is in the predigested form and contains only 0.15 per cent sucrose.

Use: Pomegranate juice may be a little more expensive than other fruit juices, but compared to other juices it is more easily digestible. The juice can be extracted by squeezing the seeds in a piece of cloth. Only sweet pomegranates should be selected for medicinal use. Pomegranate is effective in all kinds of fevers. It provides nutrition without giving any undue exertion to the digestive system.

Benefits: It is a tonic for the heart and allays cardiac pain (Wilson-Popenoe, 'Manual of Tropical and Sub-tropical Fruits', p.375). It has the power to cure vocal and mouth diseases. It has a soothing effect on the burning sensations in the stomach. It increases appetite and gives relief in anaemia. It is also very useful in diarrhoea, dysentery and coughs.

RHUBARB

Rheum emodi **Wall. (Polygnaceae)**
Amlavetasa, Himalayan rhubarb,
Indian rhubarb, Variyttu

Himalayan species of rhubarb are found wild at altitudes of 4000 to 12000 feet, in Kashmir, Nepal, Sikkim and Bhutan. The drug consists of the dried rhizome or underground stem of the plant, either whole or cut into pieces of suitable length. Rhubarb is obtained from China, and the various names of "Turkey", Russian", East Indian" etc., are merely relics of the former times when the root reached Europe from China via., the countries mentioned. Rhubarb of commerce known as "Turkey", "Russian", "Chinese" and "East Indian" is attributed to *R. officinale* and *R. palmatum*, growing in the adjacent territory of Southeast Tibet and North-western China, wherefrom it is imported into India; also imparted to a certain extent through the U.K.

Rhubarb contains a very large number of chemical substances of diverse medicinal properties and its use in western medicine at one time was well established.

Constipation: Severe—Take an infusion of rhubarb root (1 teaspoon per cup) along with ¼ teaspoon each of ginger and liquorice (increase dosage if necessary). Moderate—Take 1-2 teaspoons of Psyllum husk powder in a cup of warm water before sleep. Mild—Take 1 teaspoon of Ghee in a cup of warm milk.

SWEET LEMON

The sweet lemon, which belongs to the lemon genus, is one of the most commonly used fruits in India. Recommended during convalescence it is considered indispensable in illness. The sweet lemon with a thin peel possesses valuable nutrients.

Qualities: It is sweet, delicious and cool. It quenches thirst, is refreshing and heavy. It promotes virility but is somewhat constipating. It is very effective in excesses of wind, biliousness, cough, vomiting, dehydration, blood impurities and dyspepsia. Alkaline elements contained in the sweet lemon reduce acidity of the stomach. Its juice increases vitality and resistance power against diseases.

Analysis of Contents

Water	84.6%
Protein	1.5%
Fat	1.0%

Fruit and their Medicinal Uses

Carbohydrates	10.9%
Calcium	0.09%
Phosphorus	0.02%
Iron	0.3mg/100gm
Vitamin 'A'	26 I. U/100gm
Vitamin 'C'	63mg/ 100gm

Use: Eating the fruit cleanses and strengthens the teeth. Its fibrous elements are useful in removing constipation. However, to get the maximum benefit of its healing properties, its juice should be taken. Its juice can be easily extracted with the help of a hand juicer. Those who are suffering with colds should either slightly warm or add two teaspoonfuls of ginger juice before taking it.

Benefits: it is highly recommended when suffering with fever, especially when any other food is prohibited. During this period it proves to be a boon, providing nourishment to the beleaguered body. It also allays acidity and is an excellent appetiser. It rapidly normalises impaired digestion.

TOMATOES

Protein content 1.1gm/ 100gm

According to ayurvedic sources the tomato is light, lubricous, warm, stimulant, appetiser, laxative and removes cough and flatulence.

Analysis of Contents

Water	94.3%
Protein	0.9%
Fat	0.4%
Carbohydrates	3.9%
Minerals	0.9%
Vitamin 'A'	100 I. U/ 100gm
Vitamin 'C'	39mg/ 100gm

The tomato also contains some Vitamin 'B$_1$' and 'B$_2$'. It is rich in minerals like calcium, phosphorus, sulphur, potassium, magnesium, chlorine, sodium, iron and iodine. It also contains citric, phosphoric and malic acids, which purify the blood.

Being rich in Vitamin 'A' five small tomatoes are more than sufficient to supply the normal daily requirement. Weight for weight the tomato contains more of this Vitamin than butter. It is also surprising that the vitamin 'C' content contained in the tomato does not quickly deteriorate as in other fruits. This is probably because of the tomato's acid content. The Vitamin 'C' content increases as the tomato ripens. Only 150ml of its juice supplies one third of the Vitamin 'C' requirement for the day. Only tomatoes contain Vitamin 'B_2' and its juice is better than orange juice for children.

Uses: Tomatoes are widely used in salads, as soups and mixed in with different vegetables to enhance the taste of especially curries and other Indian dishes, it is also very popular in Italian and continental cooking, where it forms the base for many of the sauces used. It is a universal kitchen item and is found and cultivated worldwide. Its soup is obtained by boiling down tomatoes and adding various condiments to enhance the taste and its juice is also very popular. Some honey, date or jaggery may be added to tomato juice to enhance its taste and make it more palatable.

Benefits: As the tomato has a very low carbohydrate content, it is an ideal food for diabetics and for those interested in weight reduction. Its juice cleanses the stomach and the intestines. It is useful in kidney disorders, and it removes indigestion, gas and constipation. It gives relief in liver diseases. As its iron content is easily digested it is completely absorbed in the body and is thus a very important dietary addition for those suffering with anaemia. Tomato soup is also very useful for those suffering with fever.

There is a reference that in Guy's Hospital London, patients suffering with eye troubles and weakness were cured by tomato juice. In the 'Cancer hospital' in New York, the patients are given tomatoes and tomato juice.

WATER MELON

Citrullus lanatus **(Thumb) Mats. & Nakai—**
C. vulgaris Schrad. ex Eckl. & Zeyher,
(Cucurbitaceae), Creeping herb.

Tannimathan, Watermelon Fruit juice is a cooling drink with medicinal properties.
Hindi—Tarmuj

This fruit is indigenous to Africa but has spread
around the globe to become very popular in most
countries with climatic conditions suited to its
growth. Growing on a vine it is a round fruit that
attains weights varying from 1 to 12 kilograms.
The pulp is reddish in colour and very sweet in
taste.

Qualities: According to Ayurveda, the watermelon is cool, diuretic, energizing, and delicious.
It satisfies both thirst and hunger, gives nutrition
and allays biliousness.

Fruit and their Medicinal Uses

Analysis of Contents

Water	95.7%
Protein	0.1%
Fat	0.2%
Carbohydrates	3.8%
Calcium	0.1%
Phosphorus	0.01%
Iron	0.2mg/100gm
Niacin	0.2mg/ 100gm
Vitamin 'B'	2.0 microgram/ 100gm
Vitamin 'E'	1mg/ 100gm

Use: The watermelon can be eaten directly after the removing its thick rind and seeds; it can also be used as a drink in its juice form. As the juice can be consumed in large quantities the body is provided with more nutrients.

Benefits: The juice gives relief in abdominal troubles and it has a soothing effect on burning sensations in the stomach. As a diuretic, it is beneficial in kidney and bladder disorders (renal dysfunction). It is chiefly used for giving a cooling effect on the body and mind. It stimulates the process of rejuvenation going on in the body.

Fruit and their Medicinal Uses

Some more simple remedies that you can try at home using the fruit mentioned above

Constipation: *Severe*—Take an infusion of rhubarb root (1 teaspoon per cup) along with ¼ teaspoon each of ginger and liquorice (increase dosage if necessary). Moderate—Take 1-2 teaspoons of Psyllum husk powder in a cup of warm water before sleep. Mild—Take 1 teaspoon of Ghee in a cup of warm milk.

Dehydration: —To 1 pint of distilled or boiled water add, ¼ teaspoon of salt plus 3 tea spoons of natural raw cane sugar. Add 2 teaspoons of limejuice. Mix, and sip orally.

Exhaustion (*Heat*): —Apply sandalwood oil to the forehead or drink sandalwood tea. Drink coconut water or grape juice.

Gums (*bleeding*): —Apply powdered myrrh to the gums or drink lemon juice. The gums may be massaged with coconut oil.

Appetiser—Three or four teaspoonfuls of ginger juice mixed with a very small quantity of mineral salt and a few drops of lemon juice taken half an hour before meals works as an excellent appetiser.

Cholera: — A mixture of equal quantities of mint juice, onion juice and lemon juice makes a specific remedy for cholera

Abdominal troubles: —A mixture of two teaspoons of mint juice with one teaspoon of lemon juice and two teaspoonfuls of honey is a powerful medicine for abdominal troubles.

Acidity: —Take a mixture of carrot and cabbage juice. In addition to it one can take the juices of potato, cucumber, apple, mosambi (sweet lemon) and watermelon. Milk should also be taken. Avoid chillies, fried food and sweets

Acne: —Take a mixture of carrot and spinach juices. Take a mixture of potato, beetroot cucumber and grapes. Watermelon and papaya juice may also be taken. Massage papaya or potato juice on the face. Vapour bath is also very advantageous. Do not allow greasiness to remain on the face. Avoid using cosmetics.

Anaemia: —Mixed juices of leafy vegetables, beetroot, cabbage, bitter-gourd, apricot and grapes are useful in this disease.

Asthma: —Take mixed juices of carrot, beetroot and cabbage. Take a mixture of juices of leafy vegetables, or a mixture of potato and apple juices. Papaya and garlic juice can also be taken.

Bronchitis: Take warm water with ginger, honey and lemon juice in the morning, or take warm water with garlic and onion juices. Besides take radish, cabbage, beetroot, cucumber and carrot juices. Of course you should avoid smoking at all costs.

Cancer: Opinions are divided as to which juices give the maximum benefit in cases of cancer. Normally these juices are beneficial— the juices of carrot, grape, beetroot, apple, ginger, papaya, and tomato. One should try to maintain the health of the liver. Magnet therapy is also recommended.

Cardiac Troubles: Take honey, coconut water, and the juices of the papaya, pomegranate, pineapple and garlic.

Cholera: the juice of the beelee fruit mixed with the juices of mint, garlic and onion should be taken with warm water. Coconut for obvious reasons is also very useful in cases of cholera.

Cold: Lemonated warm water should be taken. The juices of ginger, orange, carrot, radish and garlic etc., can also be taken. Water vapour is also very useful.

Colitis: Take a mixture of carrot and spinach juices. Juices of cucumber, apple, beetroot, papaya, beelee and orange are also beneficial.

Constipation: in this condition raw whole fruits and vegetables are as beneficial as their juices. Proper exercises should be done. One should form regular habits in evacuating the bowels. A mixture of spinach and carrot or potato, cucumber and apple juices is indicated. One may also take fig, beelee, guava and orange juices.

Contagious diseases: on an empty stomach take warm water with lemon juice squeezed in and a teaspoonful of honey. Take a glassful of water mixed with a teaspoonful each of garlic and onion juices. A mixture of carrot and mosambi-orange juices can also be taken.

Cough: Take warm water mixed with lemon and honey every morning. Also take a glassful of carrot juice to which garlic, onion and basil juices should be added.

Diabetes: Juices of rose apple, tomato, cucumber, lemon, bitter gourd, carrot, spinach, cabbage and French beans are indicated.

Diarrhoea: Take the juices of apple, garlic and green turmeric. The juices of beetroot and pineapple are also recommended. Take complete rest.

Diphtheria: It requires immediate medical treatment. Taking pineapple juice, turn it over and over in the mouth. Do not swallow it down directly. Take warm water mixed with garlic and onion juices.

Dysentery: A regimen of thick buttermilk is one of the best antidotes to dysentery. Otherwise pomegranate and rose apple juice are both beneficial in attacks of this particular ailment.

Eczema: Take a mixture of carrot and spinach juices with a juice of mixed leafy vegetables. The juices of potato, papaya and watermelon can also be taken. Potato juice may also be rubbed on the affected area of the skin with great effect.

Eyes: Though Vitamin 'A' is very important for the eyes, other Vitamins are also equally important. One should take juices, which contain all Vitamins and calcium. A mixture of carrot juice and juices of various leafy vegetables is always beneficial for the eyes. Take care to reduce the intake of sugar.

Fever: As most Doctors do not generally recommend solid food when a patient is suffering from fever, there is really no other alternative to juices for maintaining energy. Take warm water mixed with honey and lemon juice in the morning. Warm water with garlic and onion juices can also be taken. Cabbage, gourd, basil, pomegranate, orange and mosambi juices can also be taken according to taste. complete rest is a must when you are in the grip of a fever, whether it be seasonal or connected to some other cause.

For Beautifying the Complexion: Tomato and turmeric juices, the mixed juices of beetroot and apple, guava and papaya. Cucumber juice should be drunk as well as applied externally to the skin.

For Freshness and Cooling: take the juices of watermelon, pineapple and apple.

Fracture: Fractures require the skills of qualified orthopaedic surgeons or osteopaths but as they are not always immediately available sometimes first aid is required until you can get to the fracture clinic. Where the fracture is visible it is always advisable to splint the fracture, using two rigid boards or sticks on either side of the fracture for support and to stop unnecessary movement and discomfort to the injured person whilst moving him to the doctor's clinic. A warm paste made from turmeric powder may be applied to relieve the immediate pain.

After the appropriate treatment by the doctor has been applied to aid the rapid calcification of the bones the following diet should be taken up: —A blend of six juices namely alfalfa, spinach, pot-herb, fenugreek, drumstick and bishop's seed should be taken.

Amla, watermelon, carrot, guava and papaya should also be taken. Proper rest should be given to the injured part and food containing sufficient proteins should also be taken.

Gastric Ulcers: Take about 450ml of cabbage juice daily. Also take cucumber, papaya and potato juices. Milk is also very beneficial. Citrus fruits are contra indicated. It should be realised that this condition is due mainly to the stressful lives that we tend to lead in the modern world, especially in the West. If this is the case with you try to get rid of all the mental tension and stress that you are suffering. Take to a very simple and nourishing diet and avoid as many of the condiments normally in use. Also avoid taking fibrous foods.

Gout: Take warm water mixed with honey and lemon juice. A teaspoonful each of garlic and onion juice can also be taken with warm water. The patient will also find the juices of the French bean, cherry and potato very useful. Avoid alcoholic beverages and non-vegetarian and high protein diets.

Headache: Take ginger juice, also the juices of carrots, beetroot cucumber, tomato, cabbage and apple may be taken to great effect.

High blood pressure: The juices of garlic, basil and wheat grass are very beneficial as also are the juices of carrot, beetroot, cucumber, papaya, alfalfa and orange. Avoid taking fat saturated food items like butter, ghee and vegetable ghee etc.

Impurity of blood: take the mixed juices of carrot and spinach, and the juices of cabbage, beetroot, tomato, lemon, apple and bitter gourd. A table-spoonful of turmeric juice is also very useful.

Indigestion: lemon juice in warm water should be taken on an empty stomach in the morning. Take a teaspoonful of ginger half an hour before meals. The juices of pineapple, papaya, cucumber and cabbage should also be taken on a regular basis. A blend of carrot, beetroot and spinach juices is also indicated.

Infertility: It is always necessary to find the causes of infertility. The Vitamin 'E' giving fruits and vegetables like amla, carrot, spinach, apple, and tomato etc., should be taken.

Influenza: Take warm water mixed with honey and lemon juice in the morning, or alternatively take warm water mixed with garlic and onion juices. Carrot, orange and mosambi juices are also indicated.

Insomnia: A mixture of apple, guava and potato juices as well as a mixture of carrot and spinach juices should be taken. Juice should not be taken after 6p.m.

Internal Haemorrhage: Take apple, lemon and carrot juices.

Itching eczema: By applying a paste formed from Tulasi leaves ground in lemon juice this condition can be relieved.

Jaundice: A glassful of bitter gourd should be taken on an empty stomach in the morning. Moreover the juices of carrot, gourd, beetroot, cucumber and apple are very beneficial. A mixture of papaya, green turmeric, grapes, orange and mosambi can be very profitable if taken. Chewing pieces of sugarcane and taking fresh coconut water is also beneficial. Avoid alcoholic beverages and fatty foods.

Kidney stone/s: Carrot, cucumber, beetroot, apple and pumpkin juice are all indicated. Coconut water is beneficial. Avoid the juice of leafy vegetables.

Loss of appetite: Lemon water should be taken in the morning. In addition to this bitter gourd, carrot and ginger juices can also be taken. Constipation should be relieved and plenty of physical exercise should be undertaken.

Menstrual disorders: Carrot, papaya, pineapple and grapes are all very beneficial. The mixed juices of leafy vegetables are also indicated.

Migraine: Take a glassful of water mixed with lemon and ginger juice. Perform Shakasana for 15 minutes every day without fail.

Nausea and Vomiting: There are a number of causes of this ailment. If it is due to excessive or improper eating and drinking, observe a fast for the day. Take the juices of pomegranate, papaya, lemon, orange, pineapple and tomato.

Peptic Ulcers: Excessive excretion of hydrochloric acid in the stomach adversely affects the mucous membranes and thus causes peptic ulcers. The cause of this excessive excretion is mainly put down to mental tension or worries.

Cabbage juice is a capital remedy for both duodenal and peptic ulcers. One should take 400-450ml every day. The juices of cucumber, papaya and potato can also be taken in addition to cabbage juice. The juices of citrus fruits should be avoided at all costs.

Piles: one is advised to take the juices of carrot, potato, fig and leafy vegetables. Onion juice is an excellent remedy for oozing piles. Take fibrous food in proper quantities.

Pneumonia: Take immediate medical treatment. Take warm water with ginger, lemon and honey or as an alternative take warm water with garlic and onion juices. The juices of basil, mosambi, orange and carrot are also recommended.

Pregnancy: During the period of pregnancy Vitamins 'A', 'C' and 'D' as well as sufficient quantities of iron should be consumed. One should take freely of carrot, tomato, apple, fig, beetroot, gourd and leafy vegetables.

Problems with the Teeth: For all problems regarding the teeth the juices and the solid form of carrot, apple, guava, orange and leafy vegetables are all very beneficial. The chewing of leafy vegetables and consumption of lemon juice are also very useful. Minimise the excessive use of sugar or foods that are prepared with the help of sugar like pastries, cakes and boiled sweets etc.

Pyorrhoea: Carrot , apple and guava should be eaten and well masticated. Their juices may also be taken. Lemon juice and orange juice along with leafy vegetables will also prove useful. Occasionally garlic and onion juice may be used.

Rejuvenation: All juices are useful for the rejuvenation of the body. Yet one should still be sure to take plenty of carrot, orange and spinach. Ayurveda has given much importance to amla in this regard.

Renal Diseases: All fruits are diuretic so they give relief to the burning sensations in the kidney and urinal disorders. This notwithstanding the juices of beetroot, carrot, cucumber, melon, watermelon, grapes and pineapple are the most useful in these complaints. Furthermore coconut water should be freely taken.

Rheumatism: take the juices of the carrot, cucumber, cabbage, grapes, bitter gourd, apple and coconut.

Scurvy: this disease is caused by the deficiency of Vitamin 'C'. the juices of citrus fruits and sweet fruits like amla, guava, radish, papaya, potato, lemon, orange, mosambi, pineapple and cherry etc., should be taken.

Skin Diseases:—take the mixed juices of carrot and spinach. The juices of potato, beetroot, cucumber, turmeric, watermelon, guava, apple, mosambi and papaya are also highly recommended. Potato and papaya juice can also be applied externally to the affected parts of the skin.

Smallpox:—plenty of lemonade without any sugar is useful during the fever stage.

Sinus Problems:—When suffering with sinusitis a complete cleansing of the body is required. To help cleanse the body an eliminating diet of vegetable in conjunction with fruit juices will help to relieve this irritating problem. The fruit juices best employed are orange, grapefruit, lemon, pineapple and grape. Remember these juices should neither be mixed nor artificially sweetened.

Sore eyes:—Lime juice taken every morning one hour before breakfast in a cup of hot water in conjunction with a boric acid eyewash will help to bring relief.

Splenomegaly:—Papaya juice is the most effective in this disease. In addition the juices of rose apple, lemon, green turmeric, garlic, onion and carrot should be taken.

Sunstroke:—The juices of amla and tamarind, orange and mosambi, and mixed or separated juices of melon and watermelon are all indicated.

Teething problems in children: In cases of teething accompanied with diarrhoea powdered Tulasi leaves should be administered with pomegranate syrup.

Throat troubles:—Take warm water with honey and lemon juice in the morning. Also take pineapple but allow the movement of the juice in your mouth before swallowing it. At the same time you may take a mixture of carrot, beetroot and cucumber juice. Take a glassful of warm water with a spoonful each of garlic, ginger and onion juices or an infusion of the same. A spoonful of green turmeric juice is also very useful.

Typhoid: Take a glassful of warm water mixed with honey and lemon juice in the morning or take a glassful of warm water mixed with garlic and onion juice or an infusion of the same. A mixture of pomegranate, mosambi, orange and basil juice is also recommended.

Weakened Sexual drive: the mixed juices of carrot and spinach, beetroot, cucumber and apple, and pumpkin etc.

Weight: To reduce weight take the juices of carrot, cucumber and tomato. Decrease the quantity of food consumed. To increase weight, rejuvenation by milk is most effective. In addition take dry fruits and other fruit juices.

Worms (in the gastric tract): Add a teaspoonful of garlic juice to a glassful of warm water. To this add a teaspoonful of onion juice. This mixture is very useful to one who suffers from worms. Pumpkin juice is also very effective. Alternatively a mixture of fenugreek, mint and papaya juice may also be taken to great effect.

FASTING AND HEALTHY EATING

Most major religions observe fasts as regular features of their requirements for spiritual progress. The Christians observe Lent, the Mohammedans Ramzan (both lasting for about one month) and the Hindus have numerous fasts for all occasions some more rigorous than others. It was a general practice for people to fast and pray to get victories. Quite honestly fasting has more important and useful purposes—the maintaining of a healthy body and the spiritual development of the soul. It is said that Christ fasted for forty days on behalf of humankind to gain victory over appetite. It is this very same appetite that has been guilty over generations of leading men to early graves through over-indulgence.

Fasting as a whole over short periods is beneficial both physically and spiritually. But long extended fasts only weaken one physically and therefore cannot help one spiritually either. Whilst fasting over short periods one must always be sure of taking enough liquids and one should also try to practise breathing exercises for optimum benefit. To abstain from rich food and develop the habit of taking a little plain food only is very beneficial. This gives the system a chance to clear itself of poisonous substances. Used carefully fasting is one of the best tools to enable the body to regain its balance and the mind to control its cravings for rich and harmful food. Those of weak disposition should be warned that fasting, if done at, all should be done with great care and consideration.

It is also necessary to point out that fasting may produce negative results even though you have only fasted for a few days and it is unwise to try and extend the periods of fasting unless advised to the opposite by your physician. You should therefore keep on your guard against the following complication—Kidney stones; Low blood pressure; Irregular heart beat; Gouty arthritis; Headaches or light-headedness; Abdominal pain or nausea; Decreased urine output and Severe cramps. If any of these or other complications develop then you should stop your fast immediately.

Diet plays a big part in leading a healthy and active life. It has been found that by having the proper diet and maintaining a proper life style one can have a more active and healthy life than those being far lighter in years. Health and its maintenance find its roots in both proper living and thinking. Nature has provided us with all we shall ever need to lead happy and healthy lives.

Fruit Diet

All fruits contain acid, which are necessary for the proper elimination of various toxins, poisonous acids, and other impurities. These natural acids are highly alkaline after they have been reduced in the body.

The value of a fruit diet cannot be overestimated, especially in sickness, ill health or whenever the body is filled with poisons. Germs cannot grow and live in fruit juices. The germs that cause typhoid fever and cholera cannot resist the action of fruit juices such as lemon, orange, pineapple, strawberry, apple and grapefruit. A fruit diet will disinfect the stomach and alimentary canal. Fresh fruits are more effective for this purpose than the stewed or canned fruits.

Malic, citric and tartaric acids are powerful germicides found in fruit.

Fruit and their Medicinal Uses

Malic acid is found in pineapples, apples, quinces, pears, apricots, plums, peaches, cherries, currants, gooseberries, strawberries, raspberries, blackberries, elderberries, grapes and tomatoes.

Citric acid is found in strawberries, red raspberries, cherries, red currants, cranberries, lemons, limes, grapefruit and oranges.

Tartaric acid is obtained from grapes and pineapples. Tartaric acid is important in treating all diseases that have hyperacidity, such as lung diseases, sore throats, indigestion and peptic ulcer etc.

Oxalic acid is found in plums, tomatoes, rhubarb, sorrel, yellow dock and spinach. It is especially good for both constipation and an inactive liver. But a word of caution should be given about eating foods high in oxalates. It is believed that about 10 percent of Americans will at some time during their lives develop a kidney stone, and most kidney stones are at least composed of oxalates. Therefore, if you have trouble with kidney stones you should not eat foods that have a high content of oxalates.

Lactic acid is found in buttermilk, clabber milk and soya bean milk. It is good for the treatment of fermentation and putrefaction, and in treating hardening of the arteries it is especially good.

It is best to use, fruits uncooked and never sweeten them with cane sugar.

A fruit diet is an excellent cure for chronic constipation, and is also good for reducing. Fruit gives the body strength and energy. Fruits are solvents and should always be used abundantly while on an eliminating diet.

Fruit is an ideal food. It grows more slowly than other foods and therefore it receives the beneficial effects of the sunlight and air for a longer time.

Dates, raisins, figs and many other dried fruits have become staple foods in many countries. Dates and raisins are high in natural sugar, so they are easily assimilated. Dried figs, especially Black Mission figs, are rich in the bone building elements, calcium and phosphorous as well as iron.

Orange Cleansing Diet

Drink from five to eight glasses of freshly squeezed orange juice every day. Drink the juice as soon as it has been squeezed or, if you are not so fortunate as to have fresh oranges, as soon as the container is opened. Keep orange juice tightly covered even when kept in a refrigerator. Do not let it stand exposed to the air as it rapidly loses its vitamin C content.

After taking the orange juice for five to ten days, eat a very plain, simple and nourishing diet. If the person who wishes to take a cleansing diet is undernourished and weak, and feels a little something else is necessary, eat apples, masticating them thoroughly; a few nuts may also be eaten.

If you are troubled with skin diseases of any kind, boils or carbuncles etc., a most helpful treatment is to eat eight to ten oranges a day, and drink three or four glasses of sanicle tea everyday. Take the tea after the orange juice has left the stomach, which usually takes an hour or so.

The use of herbal enemas is also suggested, but if it is found that the orange juice itself acts as a strong cathartic and causes the bowels to move several times a day then their use may be omitted after the first or second day.

The Eliminating Diet

All the good food that you may eat will not do the body any good until you have first cleansed the body by eliminating excess acid and mucus. The intestines retain these poisons, and they are one of the main causes of disease and premature ageing. By eating an abundance of alkaline or base-forming foods you can rid yourself of these poisons and acids. To correct these unnatural and unhealthy conditions and make it possible for the food that you eat to be assimilated and absorbed by the system, the body must be flushed and cleansed. Eating these foods will bring about a natural rejuvenation by constantly supplying the bloodstream with its original elements. These elements are found in natural foods, which should be eaten either raw or cooked as little as possible so as not to destroy the minerals or life-giving properties. You will be feeding the whole body not starving it. "The life is in the blood"—Leviticus 17:11. "For the life of all flesh is in the blood"—Leviticus 17:14. Health and happiness depend upon the blood stream containing all the elements necessary; when one is missing, disease in some form often results. To make the bloodstream pure and healthy, eat food in its natural state as far as possible, drink freely of pure water, bathe frequently, exercise in the pure air and sunshine, and use non-poisonous herbs.

Fruit and their Medicinal Uses

This is possible almost any time of the year anywhere worldwide, as we have fresh vegetables and citrus fruits available the year round. Just as we repair our homes or replace parts in our automobiles and other machinery so also we must take care of our bodies, supplying them with natural elements and minerals to build and repair the parts that are constantly being worn out. If pure and alkaline, the bloodstream, which provides nutrition to every cell in the body, will dissolve all poisons and carry them away. No disease can exist with a pure bloodstream.

Fruit: use all kinds of fruit liberally. All fruits must be ripe before being picked or else they will not have the eliminating qualities. Eat at least two grapefruit a day, six oranges and three lemons. Do not use cane sugar with your fruit as it destroys the beneficial aspects of the fruit. Persons wishing to eliminate who have ulcerated stomachs and cannot take fruits should drink two quarts of potassium broth a day. This is also excellent for invalids.

Vegetables: the best vegetables to use are spinach, celery, carrots, parsley, tomatoes, asparagus, mild green onions, red or green cabbage (best raw), lettuce, cucumbers, radishes, okra (lady finger), and egg-plant (bringal or aubergines) etc. eat a large raw vegetable salad each day. Cook all vegetables in as little water as possible, and if salt is necessary, use only a small amount for seasoning.

General rules whilst on the Eliminating Diet:
All the above foods, when taken in abundance, will cleanse the bloodstream. Therefore the greater the quantity taken of these foods, the sooner the body will be cleansed. Do not mistake the eliminating diet for a fast. It is in fact a feeding process. It feeds the body through the blood with the necessary life-giving minerals that everybody needs. The eating of fresh fruits and vegetables in large amounts prevents shrinkage of the stomach and intestines, and prevents lines and wrinkles from forming on the face and body.

Drink water copiously between meals.

Take moderate exercise in the open air.

Eat nothing but fruits and vegetables.

When taking the eliminating diet, do not use any of the following: —milk, cane sugar or cane sugar products, gravies, butter, free fat of any kind, macaroni, spaghetti, tapioca, corn starch, meat, tea, coffee, chocolate, ice-cream, pastries of any kind, white flour products, any kind of liquor or tobacco, bread oils of any kind, canned fruits or vegetables, potatoes, cakes, eggs, or any food that is not mentioned in the eliminating diet.

It is most important that the bowels move freely and if they do not completely evacuate at least once a day, it is wise to cleanse them once or twice a week with a herbal enema. We have five organs of elimination: —skin, lungs, bowels, kidneys and liver.

The bowel's functions will be greatly improved by these foods and the help of non-poisonous herbs.

The lungs eliminate poisons freely when we practice deep breathing and exercise.

The skin cannot eliminate poisons when it is dry and inactive. There are millions of pores that breathe and eliminate poisons. Therefore one should take a bath everyday during the eliminating process. One could even take an Epsom salts bath every other day to stimulate the skin and open the pores.

When the cells of the body are clear, they function normally and harmoniously. Thus the whole body becomes rejuvenated and the vitality is restored. Immediately after completing the eliminating diet eat sparingly of easily digested foods, such as baked potatoes, green lima beans, tender peas, corn, tomatoes and carrots etc. an abundance of oxygen helps elimination greatly. So above all be sure to breathe deeply. Use grape juice, orange juice, grapefruit juice and sweet apple juice liberally. Oxygen hastens elimination and burns up poisons.

The length of time one should spend on this diet depends entirely upon the individual. If you have been sick or eating unnatural foods for years, or almost a lifetime, you may have to follow this diet many times. Eliminate a week or longer if you are stout or overweight. At least one pound a day should be lost by faithfully adhering to this diet and that which is lost is mostly waste and poisons. If you have been habitually using drugs or patent medicines etc., the process of eliminating the poisons from your body will be longer. When all the pains and discomforts of the body disappear the poisons will have been eliminated. While they still persist you will once again have to go on this diet. It is safe for everyone to follow this diet for at least one week every month. Very little healthy tissue will be lost. The most that is lost is unhealthy tissue and waste, and the sooner you get rid of these the better it will be for your health.

Fruit and their Medicinal Uses

Table of Equivalent Fluid Measures

Gallon	Quart	Pint	Glass or Cup	Ounce	Tbsp.	Tsp. (dram)	CC (ml)
1	4	8	16	128	256	1024	4000
	1	2	4	32	64	256	1000
	½	1	2	16	32	128	500
		½	1	8	16	64	240
				1	2	8	30
				½	1	4	15
						1	4

Equivalent Weights

(Approximate)

Number of Grams	Approximate Equivalent
1000 (1kg)	2.2lb.
454	1.0lb.
100	3.5ozs.
28	1.0oz
16	1.0tbsp.
4	1tsp.

Useful household measures (approx.)

Fruit and their Medicinal Uses

Measure (ml)	Fluid ounces	Table spoonful	Fluid drams	CC
1 glassful (cup)	8	16	60	240
1 teacupful	4	8	30	120
1 wineglassful	2	4	15	60
1 tablespoonful	½	1	4	15
1 dessertspoonful	--	--	2	8
1 teaspoonful	--	--	1	4

desirable weights for men and women of 25 and over

Weight in pounds (in indoor clothing), Height in feet and inches and approximate metric equivalents in brackets.

Height '(in shoes)	Small-frame	Medium-frame	Large-frame
Men			
5'2" (158.5cm)	112-120 (50.7-54.4kg)	118-129 (53.5-58.5kg)	126-141(57.1-63.9kg)
3" (160cm)	115-123 (52.1-55kg)	121-133 (54.5-60kg)	129-144 (58.5-65.3kg)
4" (162.6cm)	118-126 (53.5-57.1kg)	124-136 (56.2-61.6kg)	132-148 (59.8-67.1kg)
5" (165cm)	121-129 (54.5-58.5kg)	127-139 (57.5-63kg)	135-152 (61.2-68.9kg)
6" (167.6cm)	124-133 (56.2-60kg)	130-143 (58.9-64.8kg)	138-156 (62.5-70.7kg)
7" (170cm)	128-137 (58-62.1kg)	134-147 (60.7-66.7kg)	142-156 (64.3-70.7kg)
8" (172.7cm)	132-141 (50-54kg)	138-152(62.5-68.9kg)	147-166 (60.7-75.2kg)
9" (175cm)	136-145 (61.2-65.7kg)	142-156(64.3-70.7kg)	151-170 (68.4-77kg)
10" (177.8cm)	140-150 (63.4-68kg)	146-160(66.2-72.5kg)	155-174(70.2-78.9kg)
11" (180cm)	144-154 (65.3-69.8kg)	150-165(68-74.8kg)	159-179(72.1-81.1kg)
6'0" (182.8cm)	148-158 (67.1-71.6kg)	154-170(69.8-77kg)	164-184(74.3-83.4kg)

Fruit and their Medicinal Uses

1" (185.4cm)	152-162 (68.9-73.4kg)	158-175(71.6-79.3kg)	168-189(76.1-85.7kg)
2" (188cm)	156-167 (70.7-75.7kg)	162-180(73.4-81.6kg)	173-194(78.4-87.9kg)
3" (190.5cm)	160-171 (72.5-77.5kg)	167-185(75.7-83.9kg)	178-199(80.7-90.2kg)
4" (193cm)	164-175 (74.3-79.3kg)	172-190(78-86.1kg)	182-204(82.5-92.5kg)

Women

4'10" (147cm)	92-98 (41.7-44.4kg)	96-107 (43.5-48.5kg)	104-119 (47-53.9kg)
11" (149.8cm)	94-101 (42.6-45.8kg)	98-110 (44.4-49.8kg)	106-122 (48-55.3kg)
5' 0" (152.4cm)	96-104 (43.5-47kg)	101-113 (45.8-51.2kg)	109-125 (49.4-56.6kg)
1" (154.9cm)	99-107 (44.8-48.5kg)	104-116 (47-52.6kg)	112-128 (50.7-58kg)
2" (158.5cm)	102-110 (46.2-49.8kg)	107-119 (48.5-53.9kg)	115-131 (52.1-59.4kg)
3" (160cm)	105-113 (47.6-51.2kg)	110-122 (49.8-53.3kg)	118-134 (53.5-60.7kg)
4" (162.6cm)	108-116 (48.9-52.6kg)	113-126 (51.2-57.1kg)	121-138 (54.8-62.5kg)
5" (165cm)	111-119 (50.3-53.9kg)	116-130 (52.6-58.9kg)	125-142 (56.6-64.3kg)
6" (167.6cm)	114-123 (51.7-55.7kg)	120-135 (54.4-61.2kg)	129-146 (58.5-66.2kg)
7" (170cm)	118-127 (53.5-57.5kg)	124-139 (56.2-63kg)	133-150 (60.3-68kg)
8" (172.7cm)	122-131 (53.3-59.4kg)	128-143 (58-64.8kg)	137-154 (62.1-69.8kg)
9" (175cm)	126-135 (57.1-61.2kg)	132-147 (59.8-66.7kg)	141-158 (63.9-71.6kg)
10" (177.8cm)	130-140 (58.9-63.4kg)	136-151 (61.6-68.4kg)	145-163 (65.7-73.9kg)
11" (180cm)	134-144 (60.7-65.3kg)	140-155 (63.4-70.2kg)	149-168 (67.5-76.1kg)
6'0" (182.8cm)	138-148 (62.5-67.1kg)	144-159 (65.3-72.1kg)	153-173 (69 3-78.4kg)

Note: Data is based on weights associated with the lowest mortality. To obtain weight for adults younger than 25 subtract 1 pound for each year under 25.

For ascertaining the height allow for a 1" heels for men and a 2" heels for women.

Calorie Table for Certain Common Foods and their usual combinations

Fruit and their Medicinal Uses

Food	Calories	Added Item	Calories	Total Calories
Bread Whole-Wheat, 1 slice	56	Butter and Jam	110	166
Milk, skimmed 1 cup	90	Milk, whole 1 cup	150	240
Salad, Lettuce, and Tomatoes	40	Mayonnaise 1 tbs.	100	140
Peas 1 cup	95	Butter, 1 tsp.	60	155
Potato, baked 1 avg., size	95	Butter, 1 tbs.	108	203
Entrée	150	Gravy	100	250
Baked apple	90	Apple pie Homemade	320	410
Total Calories	**616**		**948**	**1564**

Proper exercise is essential in any reducing programme. It doesn't necessarily have to include strenuous exercises like jogging, aerobics or swimming. Simply a brisk walk of 20 to 30 minutes thrice weekly will prove helpful and will increase the rate at which excess calories are burnt off. The following table will give you some idea of how quickly various sports or other activities burn off one hundred calories.

Minutes needed to use 100 calories during certain sports and other activities

Fruit and their Medicinal Uses

Weight of Person

Activity	155lb.	130lb.
Skiing	8 mins.	9 mins.
Swimming at 2 m.p.h.	10 mins.	11 mins.
Running	11 mins.	13 mins.
Football	11 mins.	13 mins.
Tennis	14 mins.	17 mins.
Horseback riding	16 mins.	19 mins.
Gardening	17 mins.	21 mins.
Skating	19 mins.	23 mins.
Walking rapid	19 mins	23 mins.
Bicycling	24 mins.	29 mins.
Walking moderate, 3 m.p.h.	28 mins.	33 mins.
Golf	33 mins.	40 mins.

Exercise and Calorie Expenditure

Activity (for one hour)	Calories
Bicycling at 6 m.p.h.	240
Bicycling at 12 m.p.h.	410
Cross-country skiing	700
Jogging 5 m.p.h.	740
Jogging 7 m.p.h.	920
Jumping rope	750
Running in place	650
Running 10 m.p.h.	1280
Swimming 25 yards per minute	275

Fruit and their Medicinal Uses

Swimming 50 yards per minute	500
Tennis singles	400
Walking 2 m.p.h.	240
Walking 3 m.p.h.	320
Walking 4 m.p.h.	440

From FDA consumer, July-August 1985

Here are some more suggestions on how to re-duce and maintain your weight at an optimum level. Of course please remember that if you already have a chronic health problem you should always consult your physician before you take up any regime of dieting or exercise.

1. Do not be in a rush to reduce your weight. Slow and steady is the maxim you should follow and remember you should not lose more than two ponds a week.

2. Do not eat snacks between meals if you can help it.

3. Eat a good nutritious breakfast and lunch, but go easy on supper or dinner. Do not eat just before going to bed.

4. Learn to recognise the high calorie foods and avoid them.

5. Skip desserts; eat fresh fruit instead.

6. Avoid taking second helpings however much you are enjoying the food; always leave the table knowing that you could have eaten a little more.

7. Use lots of fruit, vegetables and whole grains. These will give you a feeling of fullness whilst at the same time keeping the calorie count down.

8. Cut down on fatty foods such as fatty meats, meat products, mayonnaise, salad dressing and nuts etc.

9. Purchase and learn how to use a calorie counter. Lower your calorie intake to a point where you are losing about 1 pound a week, but never more than two pounds. *Remember you lose weight by consuming fewer calories than you use.*

10. Establish a regular exercise programme that fits in easily with your needs, and stick to it.

Normal Diet For A Healthy Person

First observe the following rules for eating: —

Diet Rules

1. Do not eat fruit and vegetables together.
2. Do not eat between meals.
3. Do not drink any liquid with meals.
4. Allow five hours between meals.

Second, more care must be exercised in the cooking of food everyday so as not to destroy the vitamins, minerals and other life giving properties during preparation.

Third, 75 to 85 per cent alkaline food should be used in the everyday diet. If you have any ailments, your diet should be at least 90 per cent alkaline base forming foods. Eating acid foods brings on disease, while alkaline foods overcome disease and help to prevent it.

Fruits

all berries	apricots	apples	pears
grapefruit	cherries	lemons	plums
pineapple	raisins	grapes	figs
quinces	bananas	prunes	dates
peaches	oranges	melons	limes

Do not use cane sugar on fruits. Do not eat bananas unless they have dark spots on the skins and are not green at the ends. Dried fruits are good as long as they are not sulphured. Do not mix more than two kinds of fruit at a meal. It is best to eat fruit raw.

Vegetables

asparagus
beets
beet tops
celery
cabbage uncooked
cauliflower
carrots
cucumbers
turnips
tomatoes
dandelions
Irish potatoes unpeeled
kale
lettuce

onions
okra (lady finger)
parsley
all kinds of greens
watercress
parsnip
pumpkin (gourd)
rutabagas
sweet potatoes
squash
Swiss chard
all sprouts
spinach
beans

Legumes

soybeansgarbanzos
green beans
dried beans of any kind

(chickpeas)
peanuts
wax beans

split peas	navy beans
lentils	string beans
lima beans	peas

Legumes are high in protein and therefore are useful as meat substitutes. As an example, peanut butter contains four grams of protein per tablespoon. The proteins contained in legumes are an adequate substitute for meat proteins if they are combined with proteins in wheat or corn products.

Approximate Time Require for Digestion (in Hours)

Rice, boiled	1 hour
Barley, boiled	2 hours
Carrot boiled	3¼ hours
Beets, boiled	3½ hours
Egg (soft-boiled)	3 hours
Egg (hard-boiled)	3½ hours
Egg (fried)	3½ hours
Egg (raw)	2 hours
Butter	3½ hours
Bread, whole wheat	3½ hours
Bread, corn	3¼ hours
Vegetable, hashed warmed	2½ hours

Fruit and their Medicinal Uses

Parsnips, boiled	2½ hours
Green corn and beans boiled	3¾ hours
Milk, boiled	2 hours
Milk, raw	2½ hours
Turnips, boiled	3½ hours
Potatoes, Irish (baked)	2½ hours
Potatoes, Irish (boiled)	3½ hours
Cabbage, raw	2½ hours
Cabbage, boiled	4½ hours
Apples, hard and sour, raw	3 hours
Apples, sweet and mellow, raw	2 hours

Some General Warnings About Herbal Drugs

Herbal Drugs don't mix with everything

Going fashionably herbal may not always be the best thing. Stay safe by following these common sense guidelines prepared by the US Food and drugs Administration.

Garlic Capsules combined with diabetes medication can cause a dangerous decrease in blood sugar. People sensitive to garlic may experience heartburn and flatulence. Garlic also has anti-clotting properties, so check with your doctor if you're on anti-coagulant drugs.

Fruit and their Medicinal Uses

Ginseng the Korean wonder herb can increase blood pressure, so it's a no-no for those battling against hypertension. Steer clear if you've been prescribed a blood-thinning drug.

Gingko Biloba, the single most prescribed herbal medicine in the world, could have serious consequences (restlessness, nausea, diarrhoea and vomiting) for those taking drugs for high blood pressure or heart disease, or even aspirin.

Guarana, the much-advertised ingredient of energy drinks like Shock and Red Bull, contains 3-5 percent more caffeine than a cup of coffee. Avoid it if you've been advised by your doctor to stay away from caffeine. Long-term use may lead to decreased fertility, cardiovascular disease and many forms of cancer.

Kava Kava, another extremely popular herb with anti-anxiety, pain relieving, muscle relaxing and anti-convulsant effects, should not be used when you've had alcohol, sedatives or sleeping pills, or are on anti-psychotic drugs and medication for Parkinson's Disease.

Statutory Warning

One of the drawbacks of opting for patent over the counter herbal medicines especially without the guidance of qualified herbalists is that, "The absence of proper quality control mechanisms to verify the ingredients and the efficacy of drugs of alternative medicines has led to the proliferation of the practice of dispensing spurious drugs containing cortico-steroids" *Dr. S K Gupta* **Head of the Department of Pharmacology, All India Institute of Medical Science (AIIMS).**

Herbal Remedy Harms

They may be spiked with steroids
They may contain allopathic ingredients
They may have toxic metals
They may result in adverse reactions
They may react with allopathic drugs

One of the golden rules of using herbal medicine is never take any herb on a regular or long term basis without the advice of qualified practitioners. Always try to use fresh herbs and avoid patent medicines wherever possible. In fact it is better to identify, grow and preserve these herbs

at home. Never use a herb unless you are abso-
lutely sure of its credentials as a healing herb.
This book is meant only as an introduction to
the world of herbal medicine and the compiler
and publisher can in no way take responsibility
for any ill effects that may occur after using any
of the remedies mentioned. If in doubt always
consult a qualified practitioner before initiat-
ing any treatment with herbs.

www.pilgrimsbooks.com

*For more details about Pilgrims
and other books published by them
you may visit our website at
www.pilgrimsbooks.com
or
for Mail Order and Catalogue
contact us at*

Pilgrims Book House
B. 27/98 A-8 Nawab Ganj Road
Durga Kund Varanasi 221010
Tel. 91-542-2314060
Fax. 91-542-2312456
E-mail: pilgrimsbooks@sify.com

PILGRIMS BOOK HOUSE (New Delhi)
2391, Tilak Street, Chuna Mandi, Paharganj,
New Delhi 110055
Tel: (91-11) 23584015, 23584839, Fax: 23584019
E-mail: pilgrim@del2.vsnl.net.in
E-mail: pilgrimsinde@gmail.com

PILGRIMS BOOK HOUSE (Kathmandu)
P O Box 3872, Thamel, Kathmandu, Nepal
Tel: 977-1-4700942,
Off: 977-1-4700919,
Fax: 977-1-4700943
E-mail: pilgrims@wlink.com.np

MORE TITLES ON HEALTH FROM
PILGRIMS PUBLISHING

The Complete Feng Shui Health Handbook
.... *Wilbelm Gerstung & Jens Meblbase*
Healing Power of Papaya .... *Barbara Simonsobn*
Ayurveda or the Hindu System of Medicine .... *B V Raman*
My Water Cure .... *Sebastain Kneipp*
Natures Remedies .... *J W Bell*
The High Altitude Medicine Handbook
.... *Andrew J Pollard & David R Murdoch*
Pocket Guide to Visualization .... *Helen Graham*
Pocket Guide to Stress Reduction .... *Brenda O'Hanlon*
Pocket Guide to Self Hypnosis .... *Adam Burke*
Pocket Guide to Aromatherapy .... *Kathi Keville*
Pocket Guide to Chinese Patent Medicines .... *Bill Schoenbar*
Pocket Guide to Ayurvedic Healing .... *Candis Cantin Packard*
Pocket Guide to Accupressure for Women .... *Cathryn Bauer*
Pocket Guide to Herbal First Aid .... *Nancy Evelyn*
Pocket Guide to Macrobiotics .... *Carl Ferre*
Pocket Guide to Naturopathic Medicine .... *Judith Boice*
Pocket Guide to to Good Food .... *Margaret Wittenberg*
Pocket Guide to Bach Flower Essences .... *Rachelle Hasnas*
Pocket Guide to 12 Steps .... *Kathleen S*
Scientific Healing with Foods, Minerals and Colors
.... *Ariel Gordon*
Therapeutic Value of Music .... *Manly P Hall*
Herb Garden .... *Helen Lyman*